Lucy M Robinson

Skyward and Back

Stories of Natural Phenomena for First and Second Grade

Lucy M Robinson

Skyward and Back
Stories of Natural Phenomena for First and Second Grade

ISBN/EAN: 9783337050474

Printed in Europe, USA, Canada, Australia, Japan

Cover: Foto ©ninafisch / pixelio.de

More available books at **www.hansebooks.com**

SKYWARD AND BACK

Stories of Natural Phenomena for First and
Second Grade

——BY——

LUCY M. ROBINSON

1895
SCHOOL EDUCATION COMPANY
MINNEAPOLIS MINN.

Copyrighted, 1895, by WILLIAM G. SMITH.
All rights reserved.

INTRODUCTORY.

DEAR SISTER TEACHER:—I send to you some stories that have given a few pleasant hours to my pupils and myself.

These are a favorite series because, my valued critics, the children, have decided in their favor. They have tried to explain, in a childish way, how, watching sun and sky and clouds touched something in their higher nature.

If you find them helpful, I ask in return that you be kind to their faults.

LUCY M. ROBINSON

SUGGESTIONS.

Have little talks that give a trend to thought and set the little eyes watching, days before, and come to the story as a natural climax. These conversations will also help the children to read with more expression, and to readily grasp the new words.

Do not attempt to read the stories continuously; but let the atmospheric changes, which to a considerable extent control the thoughts of the children, be your guide in making selections.

Do not even trouble to finish one story before beginning another, but change from clouds to sunshine, whenever it suits. This will give helpful reviews and the helpful thought that there is still something more to learn in every subject. Let some story grow that is in harmony with the day. The children enjoy songs and poems in harmony with the story and the day, and will, themselves, carry on the subject in their illustrated number and other original work.

CONTENTS:

My Sphere	7
The Sky	8
King Sun	9
The Air-Fairies	11
The Clouds	14
Queen Moon	16
The Rainbow	17
Busy Air-Fairies	18
Giant Gravitation	22
The Water-Fairies	26
The Rain-Drops' Trip	29
The Water-Fairies and Jack Frost	32
The Ground Cloud	36
The Sunset	39
North Wind	41
Cloud-Land Fairies. Part I.	45
Cloud-Land Fairies. Part II.	49
The Spruce Tree	53
Under the Snow	56
Over the Snow	58
A Winter Party	60
Who?	63
Under and Over	65
The Ice-Palace	67
Ice-Rivers	70
Icebergs	71
The Ice King	73
Baby Buds	79
A Winter Ride	82
Up In a Balloon	85
Busy Sunbeams	89
Blue Jay.—In Autumn.	94
Blue Jay.—In Winter.	96
Blue Jay.—In Spring.	98
Blue Jay.—In Summer.	100

Go forth under the open sky
and list to nature's teachings.
—*Bryant.*

My Sphere.

Look at my sphere.
It is round.
It can stand.
It can roll.
Roll, roll little sphere.
My sphere can spin.
Spin, spin little sphere.
Spin round and round.

The Sky.

Look at the sky!
The sky is blue.
The blue sky is far away.
See the sun in the sky!
The sun is far, far away.
The sun is round.
It is a sphere.
Does the sun spin?
The sun is high in the sky now.
Can you look at the sun?
No, it is so bright.
Beautiful, bright sun!
Beautiful, blue sky!

King Sun.

King Sun is far, far away.
He has sunbeam children.
He sends us the sunbeams.
They bring us light.
They make us warm.
They make us grow.
They make things grow for us.
We love the kind sunbeams.
The sunbeams have a long, long way to come.
They come very fast.
Can you hear them come?
Do they stop to play?

No, they come straight from
the sun to us.
Sometimes the clouds try to
hide the sunbeams.
They always send some
light on to us.

King Sun never sleeps.
He never gets tired.
Children sleep at night.
The sunbeams never sleep.
They go to wake up other children.
They are always busy.
They are always making new days.

The Air-Fairies.

Air-fairies float all around us.
They float in the sky, too.
We can not see air-fairies.

We can feel them fly in at the window.

We can feel them fly from the hot stove.

We can feel them when they fly fast.

Then we say, "How the wind blows."

The air-fairies whisper, "Burn, fire, burn!

We will carry heat to the children."

Could we have any fire without air-fairies?

The air-fairies say, "Grow, trees, grow!"

They say, "Children, grow;
    breathe and grow."
Could we live without the
    air-fairies?
Air-fairies say, "Little birds,
    we will help you fly."
They bring us the birds'
    songs.
They carry all the words
    we say.
We will say beautiful
    words for the air-
    fairies to carry.

The Clouds.

Look at the clouds!
The clouds are in the sky.
The clouds are white.
The clouds look soft and fleecy.
The soft, fleecy clouds float in the sky.
Can you hear the clouds float in the sky?
O, the beautiful, fleecy clouds!
See the blue sky beyond the clouds!
See the clouds hide the sun!

Can you go to the clouds?
Yes, you can go to the
 clouds in a balloon.
Can you go to the sun?

No, it is so very far away.
Some clouds are gray.
Sometimes they hide all the
 blue sky.
Some nights they hide the
 moon and the stars.

Queen Moon.

At night King Sun is gone.
He does not leave us in the dark.
He sends us Queen Moon.
He sends light to her.
She sends it on to us.
He is king of the day.
She is queen of the night.
She has stars for company.
They make the sky very beautiful.
We all love the beautiful Queen Moon.
We love the bright stars.

Look at the rainbow!
Beautiful rainbow!
See the colors! Beautiful colors!
They live in the rainbow.
Sunbeams touch the raindrops.
The colors are the raindrops' "Thank you."
Good-bye, beautiful colors.

Busy Air-Fairies.

Willie's mother stood on the doorsteps.
Little Willie stood by her.
She called,
"D—i—n—n—e—r,
d—i—n—n—e—r."
The air-fairies caught the words.
On they passed them to other air-fairies.
They made great waves of sound.
On and on to the woods they carried them.

Willie's father was swinging a heavy ax into a tree.
Into his ears the air-fairies carried the words.
He was hungry. The words made him glad.
He laid down his ax.
He held his hands each side of his mouth.
He called,
"Wh——o——o——p."
It meant, "I hear you, I'll come to dinner."
Away across the fields the air-fairies carried and passed the word.

It took many, many fairies
to carry the word across
the long field.
Every fairy helped a little.
They carried it into Willie's
ears.
They carried it into his
mother's ears.
Into the house they went.
They made everything
ready for dinner.
Soon Willie's father came.
He said, "I was glad to hear
you call when I was far
away in the woods."

Giant Gravitation.

Giant Gravitation has a home like a sphere.
Does his home spin round and round?
His home is the earth.
He has many, many long arms.
We can not see his arms.
They are very strong.
They never get tired.
The children play with Giant Gravitation.
They toss up balls.
He pulls them down again.

He pulls their sleds down hill.

Giant Gravitation pulls the children.

They say, "See how heavy we are."

They grow and grow.

He pulls hard and harder.

They say, "See how much we weigh now!"

Giant Gravitation is a good friend of the children.

He helps them swing.
He helps them jump.
He does not let them fall
off his earth.
He says, "Apples, do not go
to the sky."
He says, "Come
to earth for the
children."

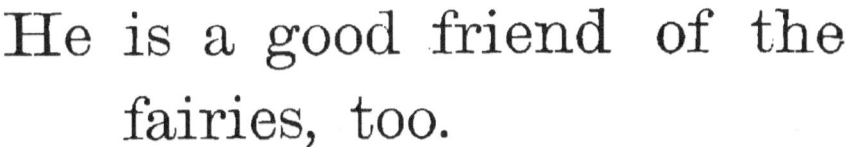

He is a good friend of the
fairies, too.
He says, "Little fairies, do
not go too far away."
He never lets any of his
little fairies get lost.

The Water-Fairies.

The water-fairies are friends of the air-fairies.
Their home is in the water.
They rest in the lake.
They run in the river.
Giant Gravitation helps them to run fast.
He wants them in his ocean.
He rocks them there.
The sunbeams make the water-fairies warm.
When they get very warm they want to fly.

The air-fairies say, "Come fly with us.
Away they fly, with their friends, the air-fairies.
They touch the grass and the trees.
They feel light and happy.
Away they fly to the sky.
They feel a cool wind.
They make fleecy clouds.
They float and float in the beautiful clouds.
Cold air-fairies fly into the clouds and say, "The thirsty trees and flowers want you."

The water-fairies fold their wings.
They cuddle into little round spheres.
Giant Gravitation calls, "Come to earth again."
Down, down come the little spheres.
They make the trees and grass happy.
The children watch the beautiful rain.

The Rain-Drops' Trip.

All the way from the sky the rain-drops wondered where they would go next.

Some of them dropped into the ground by the roots of trees.

They climbed up inside the bark and away out the long branches.

They said, "Little green leaves we have come all this way to see you."

Some of the rain-drops ran away into the earth.
They picked up bits of lime.
They crept to the river.
They carried the lime to shell fish in the river.
Some of the drops picked up salt to carry to the ocean.
Some of them crept into stones.
They hunted for things they liked in the stones.
Many together carried pebbles down the hill.

They carried tiny bits of
  earth, too.
They made a little creek.

The creek ran its way to
  the river.
The river ran on to the ocean.
All the rain-drops were very
  busy making the earth
  beautiful.

The Water-Fairies and Jack Frost.

Last night the air was full of water-fairies.

Jack Frost came to play with them.

He said, "Put on your new white dresses.

Please help me to cover the trees with frost-leaves and frost-flowers."

Oh, what fun they had!

How happy they were as they made the trees beautiful.

"Oh!" said the fairies, "we will put a velvet cover on the walks."

"Yes, and a velvet cover on the fences," said the fairies.

"The stones want a velvet cover, too," said Jack Frost.

"Oh!" said the fairies, "we will make frost-velvet and frost-flowers over everything. We will make everything beautiful while all the children sleep."

One night Ice King sent Jack Frost to say, "Winter is coming." The water-fairies grew sleepy as they heard him.

They counted one, two, three, four, five, six, and gave a push.

They were fast asleep.

Some of them pushed so hard they broke the dishes where they slept.

Some of them slept in rocks. They pushed the rocks very hard.

Some of the water-fairies
 slept in lakes.
Some slept in rivers.
They made great ice fields.
The happy children loved
 to skate on the ice.

The Ground-Cloud.

We cannot see the sunbeams this morning.
The air is thick and white.
We can hardly see across the street.
The air looks like vapor from the tea-kettle.
It looks like soft, fleecy clouds.
Why does it look so queer?
The air is full of water-fairies.
Jack Frost has made their wings white.

There are so many, they hide the sunbeams.
Sometimes the clouds hide the sunbeams.
Is this a cloud?
Are we in a cloud?
Sometimes people go to the clouds.
They go in a balloon.
They go away up to the sky-clouds.
We are not in a sky-cloud.
We are in a ground-cloud.
We call a ground-cloud, fog.
We can look into the cloud.
We can not see through it.

God can see through the clouds.
Now the cloud has gone away.
We could not hear it go.
It has gone to the sky.
Now it is a sky-cloud.
White frost-flowers are on the trees now.
Jack Frost and the water-fairies made them while the clouds were here.
Soon the sunbeams will come and pick the frost-flowers.
Beautiful frost-flowers.

The Sunset.

Willie and Alice were watching the clouds.

"See, Willie! what great mountains they make."

"Don't you wish we could climb the mountains?" said little Willie.

"I think you would need pretty big snow-shoes," said Alice.

"Oh, look, Alice! they are turning red and yellow."

"Oh, Willie, how beautiful they are!"

"Yes," said little Alice, "and I think I see castles there."
Their mother said, "They are water-fairies' castles."
"They must be very happy in such beautiful castles," said Alice.
"See how the colors change," said Willie.
"The sun is making them beautiful for us," said their mother.
"See how the castles and mountains change."
"It is a beautiful sunset."

North Wind.

Cold North Wind said, "I feel like a race to-night."
"Run away, South Wind, run fast," he said.
"I am too strong for you East Wind."
"Follow the sunset, West Wind," he cried.
"This is my night and the race is mine."
Over the mountains and over the lakes he went.
He rolled up the waves. He gave them white caps.

"Are you strong? O, trees," he cried.

He swung the branches. He tossed the leaves.

He shook off the fruit.

He shook off the nuts.

Close to the earth, the grass leaves he pressed.

He caught and carried the feathery seeds.

He scattered them far and wide.

"Have you a winter home?" he said to the birds.

"How thick is your wool?" he said to the sheep.

"How thick is your fur?"
 he said to the squirrel.
He tried the barns.
He tried the houses.

"How strong are you built?" he said.

He slammed the doors and shook the windows.

"Better drive more nails in here," he said.

He howled in the chimney.

"Get ready, Old Winter is coming," he called.

"Is your coal-bin full? Is there wood in the woodshed piled?

To-night is my night and I come to warn you all.

Get ready, Old Winter is sure to come."

Cloud-Land Fairies.

Part I.

"Sunshine, we miss you so. Oh beautiful Sunshine, do please come to see your children again. We love you, Sunshine. Where have you gone?"

"I am here dear children. I am watching the little cloud-land fairies. They are very busy and very happy fairies."

"What are the cloud-land fairies doing?

Tell us, dear Sunshine."
"They are making star-houses.
Dear little fairies, they were so happy playing with my sunbeams.
Jack Frost saw them playing.
He told the North Wind to run find them.
When North Wind touched the fairies, quickly they kissed the sunbeams good-bye.
Quickly they counted one, two, three, four, five, six.

Then they clasped their hands together, and made the star-houses.
Little cloud-land fairies love to help each other.
They are all the time helping each other."
"Where are the star-houses, Sunshine?"
"The cloud that hides me is a city of star-houses, where the fairies love and help each other."
"I wish I could see a star-house."
"You will see one soon.

When the star-house is all finished, it gets very heavy—too heavy for cloud-land.

Down, down it goes such a long, long way.

Poor frightened fairies, they do not know where they are going.

God cares for little cloud-land fairies; not one gets hurt."

"Down out of cloud-land,
　Down from the star-land,
Down into our land,
　Comes the white snow."

Cloud-land Fairies.

Part II.

"Dear little snow-stars,
   how beautiful you are.
What a long way you
   have come.
Who cared for you on such
   a long journey?
I am glad there are so many
   fairies for company in
   one snow-star.
We love you, beautiful
   white snow-stars.
We love to watch you
   come.

How softly you come.
We love to play with you.
We make you into balls.

How many snow-stars there must be in one snow-ball.
How many, many cloud-land fairies there must be in one snow-ball.

I am glad they love each other and hold each others' hands so fast.
Snow-stars, please stay with us.
Do not go back to cloud-land.
The children have been waiting for you.
The sleepy flowers have been waiting, too.
Jack Frost made them sleepy.
They laid their heads on the ground and waited for you.

Keep them nice and warm
all winter, snow-stars.
The brown grass is glad to
see you snow.
The trees are glad, too.
Keep the roots warm and do
not let the buds grow.
We are very glad to see
you dear, beautiful,
white snow."

The Spruce Tree.

How softly the snow-stars
    light on the spruce tree.
How pretty they look on the
    dark green needles.
Bye and bye the wind will
    shake them off.
Are you not glad the spruce
    trees are green all the
    long winter?
Can you see the brown cones
    hanging on the tree?
The brown cones make
    pretty winter flowers.
Don't you think so?

Do they mind Jack Frost?
Do they mind the cold winter wind?

The cones are made of scales.
There are little spruce seeds in the cones.
The cones will keep them safe and dry all winter.
In the spring they will let them fly away.
A spruce tree makes a beautiful Christmas tree.
The children hang it full of presents.
They put candles on it.
On Christmas eve they light the candles.
The children are happy with their Christmas tree.

Under the Snow.

Children sleep under a blanket made of wool.
The snow makes a blanket.
What sleeps under the blanket made of snow?
Many seeds sleep under it.
In each seed a tiny plant is waiting to grow.
The lily bulbs are sleeping under the snow.
Grass roots, full of food, are sleeping there, too.
Tiny crocus buds, ready for spring, sleep all winter.

They will not die this long cold winter.
The snow is caring for them.
The brown leaves help care for them, too.
They make a soft cover now.
They cannot frolic in the wind any more.
The toads are taking their winter nap down under the leaves and snow.
Do you know where the turtles sleep?
Woodchucks have a hole in the ground.
There they sleep all winter.

What do you know that
sleeps under the snow?
Are you glad boys and girls
do not sleep all winter?
What would they do with
their sleds and skates?
Oh, for the winter fun!

Over the Snow.

Over the snow the squirrels
frolic and leap.
The fox goes hunting his
winter food.
Have you seen rabbits' footprints in the snow?

The trees are tall and strong.
High over the snow their branches are swinging.
Some birds are here all the long winter.
Children love to go over the snow.
Sometimes they run.
Sometimes they go on sleds.
How fast they slide over the sparkling snow!
In the air the merry sleigh-bells ring.
The good horses draw their sleigh-loads safely over the snow.

A Winter Party.

Mrs. Sparrow gave a party.
Many sparrows came.
They sat on a ledge in the warm sunshine.

They said, "Chee-eep, chee-eep," to one another.
Mrs. Sparrow said, "A man had a bag of seeds.

He had them in a sleigh.
He drove around the corner.
Many seeds dropped out.
I think they dropped out
for us.
We will go and have a nice
dinner."
"Chee-eep, chee-eep, a nice
dinner! a nice dinner!"
sang all the sparrows.
Away flew the sparrows to
the corner.
How nice the seeds were for
hungry sparrows!
They heard sleigh-bells.
Very near they came.

Away flew the sparrows to let the sleigh pass.
Quickly they flew back.
They hopped about and picked up all the seeds.
Some of them flew up to the telegraph wire.
Some flew away to the roof.
Some flew back to the ledge.
"Chee-eep, chee-eep, what a nice dinner.
Mrs. Sparrow we were happy at your party.
Good-bye, good-bye."
Have you seen a sparrow party this winter?

Who?

It was very hot down there.
How all the fairies were
   working!
We rushed away.
We wanted to get out into
   the air.
We flew as fast as we could
   up the chimney.
We wanted more room.
It is much nicer up here.
We have all the room we
   want.
What fun it is to have so
   much room.

See how it makes us grow?
Do you like to see us go
 whirling away in the air?
Sometimes we make great
 puffs for you.
Sometimes we race after the
 wind.
Can you tell us from a cloud?
Good-bye, we are in a great
 hurry, we must go.
Watch and see if you can
 tell where we go.
Who are we?

Under and Over.

Under the ice the fishes are dreaming of spring.
Over the ice the merry children skate.
See the lines their skates cut in the ice.
The snails have closed their doors. They lie resting under the ice.
Near by are stalks of water-weeds they used to climb.
Lily-roots are resting.
In summer, they will give us beautiful lilies.

They will help to make us happy.
Over the ice the ice-boats glide. With white sails spread, how fast they go.
Hear the sleigh-bells ring, as merry parties ride.
Busy men are working over the ice.
They cut great blocks of ice.
They load the ice on sleighs.
The horses draw heavy loads over the smooth ice.
Busy are the winter days when they gather ice for summer use.

The Ice-Palace.

The people of St. Paul
wanted an ice-palace.
They thought it would be
so beautiful.
One winter they built it.
They cut great blocks of ice.
They built the palace with
the blocks of ice.
It took many days to build it.
They made it with turrets
and towers.
It was very beautiful.
How it glistened in the sun!
The colors were beautiful.

At night it shone clear in
the moonlight.

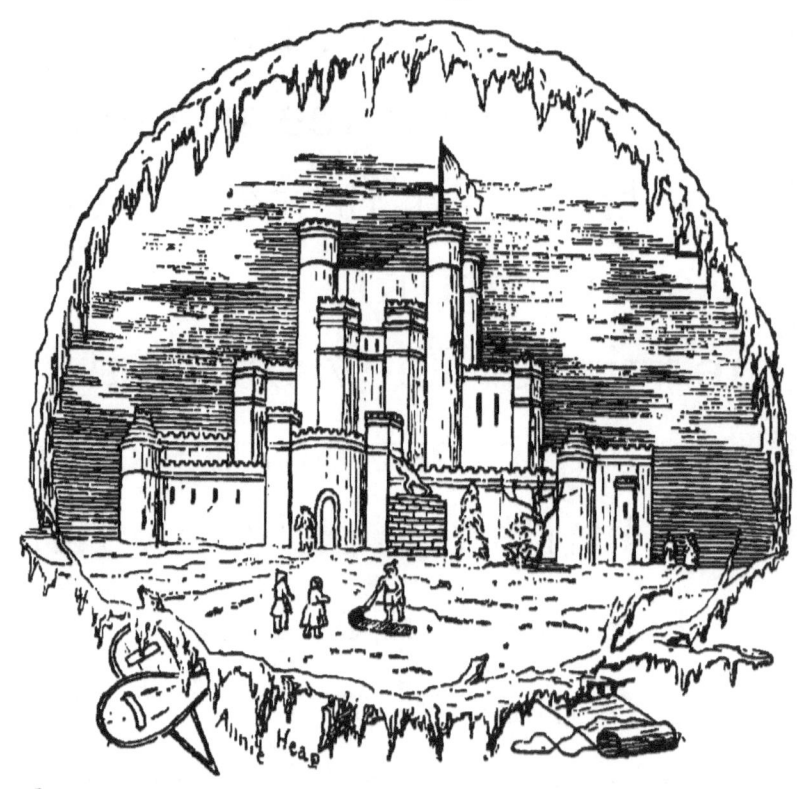

There were many rooms in
the ice-palace.
It was only to look at, no
one could live in it.
It was very cold inside.

People came from far away
to look at it.
It was a beautiful sight.
Some nights they had fire-
works around it.
The sun shone for many
days on the bright
ice-palace.
The north wind kept it
strong.
At last the south wind came
to help the sunshine.
It took many days to melt
the great ice-palace.
People like to think now
how beautiful it was.

Ice-Rivers.

Away in the far north there are ice-rivers.

They flow very slowly.

They flow between the snow-covered mountains.

Very deep are the ice-rivers.

They push very hard against the rocks.

The ice pushes very slowly onward to the sea.

It carries rocks and gravel to the sea.

It pushes great icebergs into the sea.

Icebergs.

Great icebergs go floating out to sea.
They float like great ships.
They are larger than any of the ships.

How beautiful they are.

They make the water very cold.

They make the air very cold.

They make a thick fog far around them.

Ships must not go too near the icebergs.

They would sink the ships.

Ships cannot see the icebergs through the fog.

Ships cannot see other ships through the fog.

The ships try to keep far from the fog and the icebergs.

The Ice King.

The Ice King lives in a beautiful palace.
It is on the top of a high mountain.
It is made of shining ice.
The sunbeams cover it with pearly colors.

Many water-fairies sleep in the palace.
Jack Frost visits the Ice King in summer.

His feet go click, click, click, as he walks about the palace.

He makes beautiful white ferns all about the palace.

Bye and bye the Ice King says, "Summer is gone."

Jack Frost says, "I must go down the mountain now."

The Ice King says, "Bye and bye I will follow you down the mountain."

Jack Frost goes down the mountain picking all the green leaves, ferns and flowers.

He calls to the water-fairies to help him make frost-ferns and flowers to take their places.

Then the Ice King comes out of his palace.

He walks in the crisp snow.

He walks on the ice-rivers that come down the mountain.

He loves the cold, white earth.

He never goes where he can see the green grass.

He loves the cold north wind.

"My good North Wind," he says, "drive the summer winds away."

Then he comes on down the mountain.

He crosses the rivers where the fishes sleep under the ice.

He crosses the meadows where the grass-roots sleep.

Bye and bye, the Ice King thinks he would like to go back to his palace.

The summer winds are ready to come back again.

The Ice King says, "Here are beautiful frost-flowers for you to pick.

Here are sleeping water-fairies ready to wake and welcome you.

Here are ice-rivers ready to run at your touch.

We have kept your summer treasures under soft snow-blankets and ice-covers."

Then the summer winds said, "Thank you, great Ice King. You have given our treasures a beautiful rest."

Baby Buds.

Here am I on the top of this tree.
This is my home.
Here I swing all the cold winter days.
I swung here all the bright summer days, too.
I loved the sunshine.

A green leaf shaded me.
A dear mother-leaf that
 always cared for me.
She flew away last fall.
She knew that I was ready
 to take care of myself.
I have a twin sister.
Can you find her?
I am covered with **many**
 warm coats.
They are brown and hard.
The dear sunbeams make
 them shine.
I wear my coats all winter.
Jack Frost can not hurt me.
The rain can not wet me.

Bye and bye the warm days of spring will come.
The dear roots will send me sweet sap to drink.
I shall push off my coats.
I shall hang out my fringy flowers.
I shall open pretty, green leaves.
My flowers will grow into box-elder keys.
I shall grow in the sunshine and the rain.
Now I am a bud.
In the summer I shall be a box-elder twig.

A Winter Ride.

"Dear father, I am so glad I can ride with you.
I like to ride in the woods to-day.
How beautiful the trees and the bushes are.
They seem made of glass.
Every branch has an ice cover," said Alice.
"Yes, we had sleet and rain yesterday.
That is why it is beautiful to-day," said her father.
"See how the branches bend.

They are so heavy with ice.
How they sparkle in the sun!" said Alice.

"Hear the ice crack, Alice," said her father.

"The wind is moving the branches.

Some of the ice is dropping on the snow."

"See, the snow is covered with ice, too, see how it sparkles," said Alice.

"Do you see that branch so heavy with ice?

See, it bends down to the snow!" said her father.

"It is frozen to the snow."

"I am glad it did not break," said Alice.

"Don't you think the buds need stout coats now?"

"Yes," said her father, "they need their stout coats all the cold winter. Soon the sun will melt the ice but the buds will not be hurt."

"Look!" said Alice, "mother is watching for us. Thank you, father, for taking me for such a nice ride."

Up in a Balloon.

Mr. Flammarion wanted to study the clouds.
He went to the sky in a great balloon.
He rode in a basket under the balloon.
Away, away he sailed up in the balloon.
He looked far down upon the homes.
He looked down upon the forests and fields.
Far below him he saw many lakes.

Far below him he saw the winding rivers.

Then he sailed into a cloud.
He could not see the green earth below him.
He could not see the blue sky above him.
The cloud was all around him.
He could not see through it.
He listened. He heard music from the earth.
A band was playing.
He sailed on above the cloud.
Then he looked down upon the cloud.
He looked up at other clouds in the blue sky.

It was very beautiful.
He took some birds with him.
He let the birds go.
They could not fly so high
up in the sky.
Then he floated down to the
earth again.
He sailed into the sky many
times.
He sailed among the clouds
many times in his
balloon.
He learned many things
about the air, the sky
and the clouds.
He wrote them in a book.

Busy Sunbeams.

Long ago, King Sun called his children. And all the sunbeams came.

"Would you like to go to earth?" asked King Sun.

"Yes," said the sunbeams.

"I have some presents for you to carry."

"Thank you!" said the sunbeams, "we love to carry presents."

"Here is blue for the sky," said King Sun.

The sunbeams thought the air-fairies would like the beautiful blue.

"Here is yellow, what shall we do with this color?" asked King Sun.

"May we take it to the fruits and the flowers?" asked the sunbeams.

"O yes! and they would like this red, too," said King Sun.

"We think the leaves would like the red and the yellow in autumn," said the sunbeams.

"Give them the red and the yellow in autumn."

All the sunbeams were glad to carry the red, yellow and blue.

"We must not forget this cool, beautiful green."

"It is for the grass and the trees," said King Sun.

"The grass and the trees will be happy with the green," said a sunbeam.

"Would the plums and the grapes like this violet?" asked King Sun.

The sunbeams thought they would all like beautiful violet.

Then King Sun showed them bright orange.

"What will we do with this last color?" he asked.

"We will give it to the round orange. It will be named for its color."

The sunbeams loved to carry the colors.

The children loved all the beautiful colors the sunbeams brought.

King Sun said, "I will always send bright colors for the children."

"May we always carry the beautiful colors?" asked the sunbeams.

"Yes, you may always. You may make the earth beautiful for the children," said their father King Sun.

Blue Jay.—In Autumn.

Hear Mr. Blue Jay.
He is calling "Phee-phay, phee-phay."
Nuts are plenty now.
He hides some of them.
He hides them in the ground.
He hides them in the rough bark of trees.
Mr. Blue Jay hunts for corn and peas.

He hides some of them, too.
He tastes of the apples.
He tastes of the berries.
Do you like apples and
   berries?
He likes eggs in the spring.
Do you like eggs?
The birds do not like to have
   him take their eggs.
I think he does not know
   any better.
He likes bugs.
I think you would not like
   the bugs
We like to have him catch
   the bugs.

Blue Jay.—In Winter.

Do you see that bunch of oak trees?
See the brown leaves curled with cold.

Mr. Blue Jay is hiding there.
That is his winter home.
Sometimes he flies out to hunt for food.

He finds kernels of corn
He fills his beak.
Away he flies to a tree.
He holds a kernel of corn
    with his feet.
He breaks it with his beak.
He has a nice dinner of corn.
We are glad our blue jay is
    not afraid of the cold.
We like to see his bright
    blue coat.
We like to hear his cheery
    call in winter.
We are glad to have him
    stay here all winter.
We will be kind to him.

Blue Jay.—In Spring.

Mr. Blue Jay has a pretty wife to help him.

They build a nest of roots and twigs.

Their nest is to hold five pretty eggs.

They are green eggs with brown spots on them.

Baby jays will hatch out of the eggs.

Little jays are hungry babies.

They will keep Mr. Blue Jay busy all day.

They will keep Mrs. Blue Jay busy all day.

Mr. and Mrs. Blue Jay will be very busy hunting food for baby jays.

They will watch them grow.

They will take good care of their babies.

The babies will peep, peep, their "thank you."

They will all be happy.

Blue Jay.—In Summer.

One day a baby blue jay climbed to the edge of the nest.

He had a fluffy feather suit.
He had a black feather necklace.
He gave a baby call.
He gave a baby try.
He walked on the branch.

What a proud baby he was.
He gave a hard baby try.
He flew to the next branch.
How happy he was.
Every day he flew a little
   better.
He began to hunt for food.
He learned to whistle and
   sing like his father.
He was a happy blue jay.

www.ingramcontent.com/pod-product-compliance
Lightning Source LLC
Chambersburg PA
CBHW020158170426
43199CB00010B/1088